PARTNERSHIP APPROPRIATION STATEMENTS AND CURRENT ACCOUNTS

Revision Workbook

Teresa Clarke FMAAT

PARTNERSHIP APPROPRIATION STATEMENTS AND CURRENT ACCOUNTS

BY TERESA CLARKE FMAAT

Chapter 1 – Introduction

I have written this workbook to assist students who are studying accountancy or bookkeeping. It is not designed as a teaching tool but as a revision workbook. I hope it will help you to consolidate your studies so that you can become more confident with this topic and enable you to feel more comfortable with those tricky exam questions.

In this book we will be looking at the partnership appropriation statement and the current accounts.

Topics that will be covered include:

- The sharing of profits or losses between partners
- Partners' salaries
- Interest on drawings
- Interest on capital
- Commission payable
- Partners' current accounts

It is important to note that a sole trader will normally just have a capital account, but a partnership will have capital accounts and current accounts for each partner. The capital account is generally fixed, apart from the introduction of capital and any goodwill changes. The current account continually changes and is known as a working account. It will contain items such as the share of profits or losses, salaries, interest charged on drawings, interest paid on capital, drawings etc. The current account keeps a running total of what is owed to the partners by the business.

The appropriation statement is often referred to as the partnership appropriation account. It follows on from the statement of profit and loss for a partnership business and is the 'sharing statement' for the profits of the business.

The layout of the appropriation statement will vary from partnership to partnership, so you need to be comfortable with different formats.

Example:

Kenneth and Sidney are in partnership. The profit of the partnership for the year ended 31 March 2021 is £84,000.

The partners agreed the following:
Salaries:
Kenneth   £20,000
Sidney   £15,000
Profit share:
Kenneth   75%
Sidney   25%

Using this information, we can draw up the appropriation statement for the partnership.

Hint: Imagine that we have £84,000 in a 'pot' and need to share it out to the partners in the manner agreed.

We enter the net profit from the partnership as the profit for the year. The salaries are deducted from this 'pot' to leave a residual or left-over profit which is shared in the profit share ratio agreed.

We are sharing the £84,000 in the way agreed between the partners.

Appropriation Statement

	£
Profit for the year	84,000
Salaries:	
Kenneth	-20,000
Sidney	-15,000
Residual profit	49,000
Share of profit or loss:	
Kenneth 75%	36,750
Sidney 25%	12,250
Residual profit shared	49,000

Current accounts

When the profit has been 'shared' or appropriated we can enter these amounts into the partners' current accounts. We enter these into the current accounts as money owed to the partners.
Remember: This is money we have calculated as owed to the partners, so this is a liability in their current accounts, so a credit entry. Credit entries show what the partnership owes the partners. Debit entries show what the partners have already taken, i.e., drawings, or the partners owe to the business, i.e., interest on drawings.

Current account: Kenneth

Dr	£	Cr	£
Bal c/d	56,750	Salary	20,000
		Profit share	36,750
	56,750		56,750
		Bal b/d	56,750

Current account: Sidney

Dr	£	Cr	£
Bal c/d	27,250	Salary	15,000
		Profit share	12,250
	27,250		27,250
		Bal b/d	27,250

The current accounts above show that Kenneth is owed £56,750 from the partnership and Sidney is owed £27,250 from the business.

In real life, the partners will have drawn money out during the year to live. This would also be entered into their current accounts as drawings. The drawings would be debits as these reduce the amount of money that the partnership owes them.

Let's assume that each of the partners took drawings out during the year of £10,000.

We can enter these drawings into their current accounts.

Current account: Kenneth

Dr	£	Cr	£
Drawings	10,000	Salary	20,000
Bal c/d	46,750	Profit share	36,750
	56,750		56,750
		Bal b/d	46,750

Current account: Sidney

Dr	£	Cr	£
Drawings	10,000	Salary	15,000
Bal c/d	17,250	Profit share	12,250
	27,250		27,250
		Bal b/d	17,250

You can see that the partnership business owes Kenneth £46,750 as he has already taken £10,000 during the year. And the business owes Sidney £17,250 as he has also taken £10,000 during the year.

There are a few other entries that need to be made into the current accounts and we can look at some of those now:

Interest on drawings:

This is a charge that the partners have agreed to pay for the drawings taken during the year. This is used to deter the partners from taking money out of the business too soon. Interest on drawings is charged to the partners, so the partners essentially put this back into the 'pot'.

Interest on capital:

This is a payment made to the partners for capital or money they have invested in the business. This is used to encourage the partners to leave money in the business. Interest on capital is paid to the partners just like a salary.

Commission:

This is a payment made to the partners for any commission earned in their role. Commission is an amount of money paid on top of any salary or profit share. For example, a car sales partnership may agree to pay each partner £100 for every car they sell during the year. Commission is paid to the partners.

Chapter 2 – Tasks with worked answers

Task 1:

Floki and Torvi are in partnership. The profit for the year ended 31 December 2020 is £68,000 before appropriation.

They have agreed to share the profits as shown below:

Salaries:
Floki   £10,000
Torvi   £15,000
Interest of capital:
Floki   £200
Torvi   £300
Profit share:
Floki   40%
Torvi   60%

Complete the table below to show the appropriation of the profits.

Remember:

Start with the amount of profit we must share.
Share the salaries and interest on capital to the partners.
Share the remaining or residual profit in the agreed profit share ratio.
Remember to deduct these from the 'pot' as we are taking this from the profit and giving it to the partners.

APPROPRIATION STATEMENT FOR YEAR END 31 DEC 2020	£
Profit for the year	
Salaries:	
Floki	
Torvi	
Interest on capital:	
Floki	
Torvi	
Residual profit [the profit less salaries and interest on capital]	
Share of profit or loss:	
Floki [40%]	
Torvi [60%]	
Residual profit shared [residual profit shared]	

Note:

If you are struggling with any of the maths here, try my 'Maths for accounting students' workbook.

Task 1 – worked answer:

Floki and Torvi are in partnership. The profit for the year ended 31 December 2020 is £68,000 before appropriation.

They have agreed to share the profits as shown below:

Salaries:
Floki   £10,000
Torvi   £15,000

Interest of capital:
Floki   £200
Torvi   £300

Profit share:
Floki   40%
Torvi   60%

Complete the table below to show the appropriation of the profits.

Remember:

Start with the amount of profit we must share.
Share the salaries and interest on capital to the partners.
Share the remaining or residual profit in the agreed profit share ratio.
Remember to deduct these from the 'pot' as we are taking this from the profit and giving it to the partners.

The net profit is entered in 'profit for the year'.
This money is then shared in the ways agreed.
Deduct the salaries from the 'pot'.
Deduct the interest on capital from the 'pot'.
Calculate the residual profit that is left after these monies have been shared.
Share the profit or loss using the percentages given.
Add the profits shared together and enter this as the 'residual profit shared'.

APPROPRIATION STATEMENT FOR YEAR END 31 DEC 2020	£
Profit for the year	68,000
Salaries:	
Floki	-10,000
Torvi	-15,000
Interest on capital:	
Floki	-200
Torvi	-300
Residual profit [the profit less salaries and interest on capital]	42,500
Share of profit or loss:	
Floki [40%]	17,000
Torvi [60%]	25,500
Residual profit shared	42,500

Task 2:

Ragnar and Ivar are in partnership. The appropriation statement for their partnership is below.

APPROPRIATION STATEMENT FOR RAGNAR AND IVAR	£
Profit for the year	130,000
Salaries:	
Ragnar	-25,000
Ivar	-20,000
Interest on capital:	
Ragnar	-1,000
Ivar	-1,000
Interest charged on drawings:	
Ragnar	200
Ivar	500
Residual profit	83,700
Share of profit or loss:	
Ragnar	41,850
Ivar	41,850
Residual profit shared	83,700

You are also told that the following drawings were taken by the partners during the year:

Ragnar: £20,000
Ivar: £50,000

Complete the partners current accounts with the information shown above.

Note: There are opening balances in the partners' current accounts.

Current account: Ragnar

Dr	£	Cr	£
		Bal b/d	1,200

Current account: Ivar

Dr	£	Cr	£
		Bal b/d	800

Task 2: worked answer

Ragnar and Ivar are in partnership. The appropriation statement for their partnership is below.

APPROPRIATION STATEMENT FOR RAGNAR AND IVAR	£
Profit for the year	130,000
Salaries:	
Ragnar	-25,000
Ivar	-20,000
Interest on capital:	
Ragnar	-1,000
Ivar	-1,000
Interest charged on drawings:	
Ragnar	200
Ivar	500
Residual profit	83,700
Share of profit or loss:	
Ragnar	41,850
Ivar	41,850
Residual profit shared	83,700

You are also told that the following drawings were taken by the partners during the year:
Ragnar: £20,000
Ivar: £50,000

Complete the partners current accounts with the information shown above.
Note: There are opening balances in the partners' current accounts.

Enter all the amounts due to the partners as credits as these are owed to the partners when the profit is shared.

Enter all the amounts due from the partners or already taken as debits.

Balance the accounts to calculate how much each partner is still owed by the partnership.

Current account: Ragnar

Dr	£	Cr	£
Drawings	20,000	Bal b/d	1,200
Interest on drawings	200	Salary	25,000
Bal c/d	48,850	Interest on capital	1,000
		Profit share	41,850
	69,050		69,050
		Bal b/d	48,850

Current account: Ivar

Dr	£	Cr	£
Drawings	50,000	Bal b/d	800
Interest on drawings	500	Salary	20,000
Bal c/d	13,150	Interest on capital	1,000
		Profit share	41,850
	63,650		63,650
		Bal b/d	13,150

Task 3:

Complete the following sentences:

a) Interest on capital is *paid to/charged to* the partners' current accounts.

b) Interest on capital is entered as a *debit/credit* in the partners' current accounts.

c) Profit share is entered as a *debit/credit* in the partners' current accounts.

d) Interest on drawings is *paid to/charged to* the partners' current accounts.

e) The share of a loss is entered as a **debit/credit** in the partners' current accounts.

f) The appropriation statement follows on from the partnership *statement of profit and loss/statement of financial position.*

Task 3: answers

Complete the following sentences:

a) Interest on capital is ***(paid to)**/charged to* the partners' current accounts.

b) Interest on capital is entered as a ***debit/(credit)*** in the partners' current accounts.

c) Profit share is entered as a ***debit/(credit)*** in the partners' current accounts.

d) Interest on drawings is ***paid to/(charged to)*** the partners' current accounts.

e) The share of a loss is entered as a **(debit)/credit** in the partners' current accounts. **This one was tricky! But remember the partner would receive a share of a profit, so would need to pay back the share of a loss, so this is deducted from their current account balance.**

f) The appropriation statement follows on from the partnership ***(statement of profit and loss)/statement of financial position***.

Chapter 3 – Tasks

Answers to these tasks, with workings, are given at the back of the workbook.

Task 4:

George and Tammy are in partnership. You have been provided with the following information.

The net profit for the year ended 31 March 2021 was £83,000 before appropriations.

	George	Tammy
Profit share	70%	30%
Interest on capital per year	£800	£1,300
Salary per annum (year)	£36,000	£14,000
Drawings in the year	£20,000	£16,000
Interest on drawings	£200	£160

Prepare the appropriation statement for the partnership by completing the table below.

Hint: Share the money due to the partners by deducting it from the net profit and add back anything they are charged. When you have calculated the remaining profit, the residual profit, share this using the profit share ratio.

Remember: You are only sharing the profit – drawings are dealt with in the current accounts.

Note: The format in this one is different, but the entries are the same.

Appropriation statement	£
Profit for appropriation	
Interest on capital: George	
Interest on capital: Tammy	
Interest on drawings: George	
Interest on drawings: Tammy	
Salary: George	
Salary: Tammy	
Residual profit	
Profit share: George	
Profit share: Tammy	
Total residual profit shared	

Task 5:

Sharna and Tom are in partnership sharing profits in the ratio of 3:2.

The profit from the partnership for this year is £55,000.

The balance on their current accounts at the end of last year were:

Sharna: £3,000 credit

Tom: £500 debit

Complete the current accounts below, clearly showing the balance b/d.

Current account: Sharna

Dr	£	Cr	£

Current account: Tom

Dr	£	Cr	£

Task 6:

Pavlina, Tracey and Maha are in partnership. You have been provided with the following information about the partnership.

PTM Partnership for the year ended 31 March 2021.

	Pavlina	Tracey	Maha
Profit share ratio	40%	40%	20%
Capital account balance	£80,000	£60,000	£30,000
Salary per month	£1,500	£2,000	£1,500

You are also told that interest is paid on capital balances at a rate of 2%.

The net profit for the year was £96,000.

Complete the appropriation statement below for the PTM Partnership.

Note: The salary is given per month! You need to calculate it for the year.

Appropriation statement	Total £	Pavlina £	Tracey £	Maha £
Profit for appropriation	96,000			
Interest on capital	3,400	1,600	1,200	600
Salaries	60,000	18,000	24,000	18,000
Residual profit	32,600			
Profit share		13,040	13,040	6,520
Totals		32,640	38,240	25,120

Task 7:

Ron and Joan have been in partnership for many years sharing profits equally. The profit for the year ended 31 December 2020 was £76,000.

They have agreed the following for the last financial year.

	Ron £	Joan £
Salaries	£15,000	£20,000
Commission payable	£1,400	£3,000
Interest charged on drawings	£200	£400

You are also told that drawings have been made during the year of the following:
Ron: £20,000
Joan: £40,000

Complete the appropriation statement below and transfer the totals to the current accounts.

Note: The bal b/d from the previous year has already been entered into the current accounts.

Appropriation statement	Totals £	Ron £	Joan £
Profit for appropriation			
Salaries			
Commission payable			
Interest charged on drawings			
Residual profit			
Profit share			
Totals			

PARTNERSHIP APPROPRIATION STATEMENTS AND CURRENT ACCOUNTS

Current account: Ron

Dr	£	Cr	£
		Bal b/d	2,000

Current account: Joan

Dr	£	Cr	£
		Bal b/d	1,500

Task 8:

Shaun and Ewa have provided you with the following appropriation statement for the financial year to 31 March 2021.

Appropriation statement for Shaun and Ewa 31/03/2021	£
Profit for appropriation	60,000
Interest on capital: Shaun	-500
Interest on capital: Ewa	-1,000
Interest on drawings: Shaun	360
Interest on drawings: Ewa	500
Salary: Shaun	-5,000
Salary: Ewa	-20,000
Residual profit	34,360
Profit share:	22,907
Profit share:	11,453

You have also been told that each partner took drawings through the year with Shaun taking £18,000 and Ewa taking £25,000.

Complete the current accounts below clearly showing the bal c/d and bal b/d for each partner.

Note: The current accounts have been merged into one ledger here, so be careful to enter the figures into the current columns.
The opening balances have already been entered.

Hint: It is sometimes easier to complete the current account for one partner at a time.

Current accounts

Dr	Shaun £	Ewa £	Cr	Shaun £	Ewa £
Bal b/d	500		Bal b/d		3,500

Task 9:

You have been provided with the following details about a partnership business.

- The partners are Lennox and Simone.
- The financial year ends 31 December 2020.
- The profit for the year was £72,000.
- There is no interest on capital or drawings.
- Lennox and Simone share profits in the ratio of 6:4.
- Lennox is entitled to a salary of £12,000.
- Simone is entitled to a salary of £18,000.
- Lennox earned sales commission of £5,000 through the year.
- Lennox took drawings of £15,000.
- Simone took drawings of £22,000.

Prepare the appropriation statement for the partnership for the year ended 31 December 2020 and complete the partners' current accounts.

	Totals £	Lennox £	Simone £
Profit for appropriation			
Salaries			
Commission			
Residual profit for distribution			
Profit share			
Balance			

Current account: Lennox

Dr	£	Cr	£
		Bal b/d	3,000

Current account: Simone

Dr	£	Cr	£
Bal b/d	12,000		

Task 10:

Pauline and Geoff are in partnership. They have provided you with the following information.

Net profit for the partnership for the year ended 31 March 2021 was £95,000.

	Pauline	Geoff
Capital account balances	£50,000	£60,000
Current account balances	£2,100 debit	£1,800 credit
Profit share ratio	70%	30%
Salaries	£22,000	£14,000
Interest on capital	1.5% of balance	1.5% of balance
Drawings	£40,000	£30,000

You are required to prepare the appropriation statement and current accounts for Pauline and Geoff.

Note: The current account balances are given but have not yet been entered in the current accounts.

The interest on capital needs to be calculated by multiplying the capital account balance by the interest on capital percentage.

PARTNERSHIP APPROPRIATION STATEMENTS AND CURRENT ACCOUNTS

Appropriation statement	Totals £	Pauline £	Geoff £
Profit for appropriation			
Salaries			
Interest on capital			
Residual profit			
Profit share			
Totals			

Current account: Pauline

Dr	£	Cr	£

Current account: Geoff

Dr	£	Cr	£

PARTNERSHIP APPROPRIATION STATEMENTS AND CURRENT ACCOUNTS

Task 11:

Below is the statement of financial position for Joey and Tiger.

You are told that the capital balances at 31 March 2021 were:

Joey: £50,000 and Tiger £50,000

The profit for the year was £66,000 and the partners share the profits equally.

The balances on the current accounts on 1 April 2020 (start of the year) were:

Joey: £6,000 credit

Tiger: £2,000 debit

Drawings were taken during the year of:

Joey: £18,000

Tiger: £26,500

You are required to complete the "represented by" section at the bottom of the statement of financial position.

Hint:

You already have the capital account balances, but you will need to calculate the balances of the current accounts.

You might find it useful to draw the current accounts first, even though they may not be part of the question. It will help to avoid errors.

Two blank ones are here for you to use:

PARTNERSHIP APPROPRIATION STATEMENTS AND CURRENT ACCOUNTS

Current account:...........................

Dr	£	Cr	£

Current account:...........................

Dr	£	Cr	£

Statement of Financial Position for JT Partnership at 31 March 2021

Non-current assets:	Cost	Acc. Depreciation	Carrying amount
Machinery	£80,000	£12,000	£68,000
Current assets:			
Bank	£24,000		
SLCA	£42,000		
Inventory	£15,000	£81,000	
Current liabilities:			
PLCA	£22,000		
Accruals	£ 1,500	£23,500	
Net current assets:			£57,500
Net assets:			£125,500

Represented by:

	Joey £	Tiger £	Totals £
Capital accounts			
Current accounts			
Totals			

Task 12:

True or False?

	True	False
Interest paid on capital balances is credited to the partners' current accounts.		
Profits are always shared equally between partners in the appropriation statement.		
The appropriation statement follows the partnership statement of profit and loss.		
Appropriation statements are used for sole traders and partnerships.		
Interest charged on drawings is credited to the partners' current accounts.		
Commission paid to partners is credited to their capital accounts.		
Current account balances appear in the 'represented by' section at the bottom of the statement of financial position.		
Drawings are debited to the partners' current accounts.		
Profit shares are credited to the partners' current accounts.		
A credit balance in a partner's current account represents money owed to the partner from the partnership.		

Task 13:

You have been provided with the following information about a partnership business.

- The partners are Ana, Will and Jordan
- The financial year end is 31 March 2021.
- The profit for the year was £78,000 before appropriations.
- The partners salaries are Ana £35,000, Will £30,000, Jordan £22,000.
- The partners interest on capital are Ana £1,000, Will £1,200, Jordan £1,500.
- The partners interest on drawings are Ana £200, Will £300, Jordan £400.
- The profit share ratio is 4:4:2.

Complete the appropriation statement below for the partnership.

Hint: If you are left with a residual loss, you need to share this in the same ratio that you would share the profit.

Note: The appropriation statements may be laid out differently, but the content is basically the same.

PARTNERSHIP APPROPRIATION STATEMENTS AND CURRENT ACCOUNTS

	Total £	Ana £	Will £	Jordan £
Profit for the year				
Residual profit or loss for distribution				
Share of residual profit or loss				
Total profit shared				

Check your answers by totalling the partner columns. These should match the total profit for the year.

Task 14:

Zoe and Ben have been in partnership for several years sharing profit equally.

The partnership agreement states that Zoe receives a salary of £20,000 and Ben receives a salary of £25,000.

Both partners receive interest on capital at 10% of their capital account balances at the year-end.

The capital balances at the year-end were: Zoe £50,000, Ben £80,000.

During the year Zoe took out £15,000 in drawings and Ben took out £20,000 in drawings. Interest is charged on drawings at a rate of 5%.

The balances on their current accounts at the start of the year were: Zoe £3,000 credit, Ben £4,000 debit.

The profit for the year was £98,000.

a) Complete the appropriation statement below for the partnership.

Remember: The appropriation statement may be in a different format, but the content is the same.

PARTNERSHIP APPROPRIATION STATEMENTS AND CURRENT ACCOUNTS

	Total £
Profit for the year	
Interest on capital:	
Salaries:	
Interest on drawings:	
Residual profit or loss for distribution	
Profit shares:	
Total residual profit or loss distributed	

b) Complete the partners current accounts below.

Current account: Zoe

Dr	£	Cr	£

Current account: Ben

Dr	£	Cr	£

Task 15:

a) Profits of a two-person partnership are £40,000.

Total interest on capital accounts is £3,000.

Total salaries are £18,000.

If the remaining profits are shared equally, how much will each partner's share of the residual profit be?

b) Profits of a two-person partnership are £62,000.

Total interest on capital accounts is £4,000.

Total interest on drawings is £2,500.

Total salaries are £20,000.

If the remaining profits are shared equally, how much will each partner's share of the residual profit be?

c) Paula and Zenildo are in partnership sharing profits and losses in the ratio of 3:2.

The opening balances in their current accounts are:

Paula: £4,000 credit

Zenildo: £1,800 debit

The profit for the year is £63,000 and there are no other appropriations.

Calculate the closing balances of the partners current accounts after the profit has been shared.

Paula

Zenildo

Task 16:

Answer the following questions in your own words.

a) Explain what drawings from a partnership are.

b) Explain why interest on drawings is charged to partners.

c) Explain why interest on capital is paid to partners.

d) Explain why current accounts are kept for partners.

e) Explain what a partnership appropriation statement is for.

f) Explain what a credit balance in a current account means for the partner.

g) Explain what a debit balance in a current account means for the partner.

h) Explain how a profit share ratio is decided.

Chapter 4 - Answers

Task 4:

George and Tammy are in partnership. You have been provided with the following information.

The net profit for the year ended 31 March 2021 was £83,000 before appropriations.

	George	Tammy
Profit share	70%	30%
Interest on capital per year	£800	£1,300
Salary per annum (year)	£36,000	£14,000
Drawings in the year	£20,000	£16,000
Interest on drawings	£200	£160

Prepare the appropriation statement for the partnership by completing the table below.

Start by entering the profit available for appropriation or sharing.

Share the interest on capital by taking this from the profit pot.

Add back the interest on drawings by adding this to the profit pot, because this is money the partners need to pay back to the partnership.

Share the salaries by taking this from the profit pot.

Calculate what is left in the pot, the residual profit.

Share the profit as agreed, with George getting 70% and Tammy 30%.

Total the residual profit shared to check your calculations.

Appropriation statement	£
Profit for appropriation	83,000
Interest on capital: George	-800
Interest on capital: Tammy	-1,300
Interest on drawings: George	200
Interest on drawings: Tammy	160
Salary: George	-36,000
Salary: Tammy	-14,000
Residual profit	31,260
Profit share: George	21,882
Profit share: Tammy	9,378
Total residual profit shared	31,260

Task 5:

Sharna and Tom are in partnership sharing profits in the ratio of 3:2.

The profit from the partnership for this year is £55,000.

The balance on their current accounts at the end of last year were:

Sharna: £3,000 credit

Tom: £500 debit

Complete the current accounts below, clearly showing the balance b/d.

Start by entering the balance brought down from last year. Note that Sharna's balance is a credit and Tom's balance is a debit. This means that the partnership still owed Sharna some money, but Tom had taken a little too much, so owed it back to the partnership at the start of the year.

Transfer each partner's share of the profit into their current account using the ratio 3:2.

<u>Remember:</u> **To work out the ratio, add up the total portions (3 + 2), then divide the profit by the total portions and multiply by each partner's share.**

£55,000 / 5 = £11,000 x 3 = £33,000

£55,000 / 5 = £11,000 x 2 = £22,000.

Balance off the accounts by entering the bal c/d and then the bal b/d.

Current account: Sharna

Dr	£	Cr	£
Bal c/d	36,000	Bal b/d	3,000
		Profit share	33,000
	36,000		36,000
		Bal b/d	36,000

Current account: Tom

Dr	£	Cr	£
Bal b/d	500	Profit share	22,000
Bal c/d	21,500		
	22,000		22,000
		Bal b/d	21,500

Task 6:

Pavlina, Tracey and Maha are in partnership. You have been provided with the following information about the partnership.

PTM Partnership for the year ended 31 March 2021.

	Pavlina	Tracey	Maha
Profit share ratio	40%	40%	20%
Capital account balance	£80,000	£60,000	£30,000
Salary per month	£1,500	£2,000	£1,500

You are also told that interest is paid on capital balances at a rate of 2%.

The net profit for the year was £96,000.

Complete the appropriation statement below for the PTM Partnership.

Enter the profit available for appropriation or sharing.

Enter the interest payable on the capital balances. You will need to calculate this first.
£80,000 / 100 x 2 = £1,600
£60,000 / 100 x 2 = £1,200
£30,000 / 100 x 2 = £600

Enter the salaries for the year, so multiply the monthly salary by 12. Work out the residual profit available to share in the profit share ratio. Total the columns to check your calculations. Your totals should add up to the total profit available for appropriation, £96,000.

Appropriation statement	Total £	Pavlina £	Tracey £	Maha £
Profit for appropriation	96,000			
Interest on capital	-3,400	1,600	1,200	600
Salaries	-60,000	18,000	24,000	18,000
Residual profit	32,600			
Profit share	-32,600	13,040	13,040	6,520
Totals		32,640	38,240	25,120

Task 7:

Ron and Joan have been in partnership for many years sharing profits equally. The profit for the year ended 31 December 2020 was £76,000.

They have agreed the following for the last financial year.

	Ron £	Joan £
Salaries	£15,000	£20,000
Commission payable	£1,400	£3,000
Interest charged on drawings	£200	£400

You are also told that drawings have been made during the year of the following:
Ron: £20,000
Joan: £40,000

Complete the appropriation statement below and transfer the totals to the current accounts.

Note: The bal b/d from the previous year has already been entered into the current accounts.

The profit to be shared is entered as the profit for appropriation. The salaries are taken from the profit pot and given to the partners.

The salaries are taken from the profit pot and given to the partners.

The interest on drawings is added back to the profit pot and charged to the partners.

The residual profit, or the amount left in the profit pot, is then shared equally between the partners as agreed.

Appropriation statement	Totals £	Ron £	Joan £
Profit for appropriation	76,000		
Salaries	-35,000	15,000	20,000
Commission payable	-4,400	1,400	3,000
Interest charged on drawings	600	-200	-400
Residual profit	37,200		
Profit share	-37,200	18,600	18,600
Totals		34,800	41,200

The details from the appropriation statement are entered into the current accounts.

The salaries, commission and profit share are all owed to the partners so are entered as credits (liabilities to the business).

The interest on drawings and drawings are owed by the partners to the business so are entered as debits (assets to the business).

The accounts are balanced to calculate the new balance b/d for each partner.

Note: The balances could be on either side of the current accounts depending on whether the partnership owes the partner, or the partner owes the partnership.

Current account: Ron

Dr	£	Cr	£
Interest on drawings	200	Bal b/d	2,000
Drawings	20,000	Salary	15,000
Bal c/d	16,800	Commission	1,400
		Profit share	18,600
	37,000		37,000
		Bal b/d	16,800

Current account: Joan

Dr	£	Cr	£
Interest on drawings	400	Bal b/d	1,500
Drawings	40,000	Salary	20,000
Bal c/d	2,700	Commission	3,000
		Profit share	18,600
	43,100		43,100
		Bal b/d	2,700

Task 8:

Shaun and Ewa have provided you with the following appropriation statement for the financial year to 31 March 2021.

Appropriation statement for Shaun and Ewa 31/03/2021	£
Profit for appropriation	60,000
Interest on capital: Shaun	-500
Interest on capital: Ewa	-1,000
Interest on drawings: Shaun	360
Interest on drawings: Ewa	500
Salary: Shaun	-5,000
Salary: Ewa	-20,000
Residual profit	34,360
Profit share:	22,907
Profit share:	11,453

You have also been told that each partner took drawings through the year with Shaun taking £18,000 and Ewa taking £25,000.

Complete the current accounts below clearly showing the bal c/d and bal b/d for each partner.

Note: The current accounts have been merged into one ledger here, so be careful to enter the figures into the current columns.
The opening balances have already been entered.

Hint: It is sometimes easier to complete the current account for one partner at a time.

PARTNERSHIP APPROPRIATION STATEMENTS AND CURRENT ACCOUNTS

The balances brought down were already entered, so don't forget to include these in your calculations.
Enter the interest owed to the partners on the credit side.
Enter the salaries owed to the partners on the credit side.
Enter the profit share owed to the partners on the credit side.
Enter the interest on drawings charged to the partners on the debit side.
Enter the drawings already taken by the partners on the debit side.
Balance off each partner's accounts in turn to calculate the bal c/d and bal b/d.

Current accounts

Dr	Shaun £	Ewa £	Cr	Shaun £	Ewa £
Bal b/d	500		Bal b/d		3,500
Int. on drawings	360	500	Int. on capital	500	1,000
Drawings	18,000	25,000	Salary	5,000	20,000
Bal c/d	9,547	10,453	Profit share	22,907	11,453
	28,407	35,953		28,407	35,953
			Bal b/d	9,547	10,453

Task 9:

You have been provided with the following details about a partnership business.

- The partners are Lennox and Simone.
- The financial year ends 31 December 2020.
- The profit for the year was £72,000.
- There is no interest on capital or drawings.
- Lennox and Simone share profits in the ratio of 6:4.
- Lennox is entitled to a salary of £12,000.
- Simone is entitled to a salary of £18,000.
- Lennox earned sales commission of £5,000 through the year.
- Lennox took drawings of £15,000.
- Simone took drawings of £22,000.

Prepare the appropriation statement for the partnership for the year ended 31 December 2020 and complete the partners current accounts.

This question has put all the information into sentences, but the information is the same as those which are given in a table format.
Enter the profit available for appropriation.
Take out the entitlements such as salary and commission and give them to the partners.
Work out the residual profit available and share this in the ratio given in the information.
To check your answer the balances in Lennox and Simone's columns should equal the profit available for appropriation, the £72,000.

PARTNERSHIP APPROPRIATION STATEMENTS AND CURRENT ACCOUNTS

	Totals £	Lennox £	Simone £
Profit for appropriation	72,000		
Salaries	-30,000	12,000	18,000
Commission	-5,000	5,000	0
Residual profit for distribution	37,000		
Profit share		22,200	14,800
Balance		39,200	32,800

Take the information from the appropriation statement and enter those details into the current accounts for the partners.

The balance b/d has already been entered.

The salary, commission and profit share are owed to the partners, so these are credit entries.

Enter the drawings already taken by the partners. Drawings are a debit because they reduce what the partnership owes to the partners.

Total each of the current accounts in turn. Note that the balance c/d can be on either side.

Current account: Lennox

Dr	£	Cr	£
Drawings	15,000	Bal b/d	3,000
Bal c/d	27,200	Salary	12,000
		Commission	5,000
		Profit share	22,200
	42,200		42,200
		Bal b/d	27,200

Current account: Simone

Dr	£	Cr	£
Bal b/d	12,000	Salary	18,000
Drawings	22,000	Profit share	14,800
		Bal c/d	1,200
	34,000		34,000
Bal b/d	1,200		

<u>Note:</u> Simone's balance brought down is on the debit side which means that the partner owes this back to the partnership, as she has taken more than her entitlement. This remains an asset to the partnership.

Lennox's balance brought down is on the credit side which means that the partner is owed this money by the partnership, as he has not taken everything that he was entitled to. This remains a liability to the partnership.

Task 10:

Pauline and Geoff are in partnership. They have provided you with the following information.

Net profit for the partnership for the year ended 31 March 2021 was £95,000.

	Pauline	Geoff
Capital account balances	£50,000	£60,000
Current account balances	£2,100 debit	£1,800 credit
Profit share ratio	70%	30%
Salaries	£22,000	£14,000
Interest on capital	1.5% of balance	1.5% of balance
Drawings	£40,000	£30,000

You are required to prepare the appropriation statement and current accounts for Pauline and Geoff.

Note: The current account balances are given but have not yet been entered in the current accounts.

The interest on capital needs to be calculated by multiplying the capital account balance by the interest on capital percentage.

PARTNERSHIP APPROPRIATION STATEMENTS AND CURRENT ACCOUNTS

Enter the details into the appropriation statement as you have done in previous tasks.

This time you need to calculate the interest on capital.

£50,000 / 100 = £500 x 1.5 = £750

£60,000 / 100 = £600 x 1.5 = £900

Share the residual profit 70% to Pauline and 30% to Geoff.

Use whatever method you find easiest to calculate percentages.

You can either enter the residual profit into the calculator and multiply by 70% and 30%.

Or you take enter the residual profit into the calculator, divide by 100 to find 1%, and then multiply that by 70 and then 30.

Appropriation statement	Totals £	Pauline £	Geoff £
Profit for appropriation	95,000		
Salaries	-36,000	22,000	14,000
Interest on capital	-1,650	750	900
Residual profit	57,350		
Profit share	-57,350	40,145	17,205
Totals		62,895	32,105

When you have completed the appropriation statement start the current accounts by entering in the balances given in the question.

Note that Pauline's balance is a debit and Geoff's balance is a credit. Take time in a question to double-check this.

PARTNERSHIP APPROPRIATION STATEMENTS AND CURRENT ACCOUNTS

Make entries for all the entitlements of the partners by crediting these to their current accounts.

Make entries for the drawings on the debit side to reduce what the partnership owes each partner.

Balance off the account and show the bal c/d and bal b/d.

Current account: Pauline

Dr	£	Cr	£
Bal b/d	2,100	Salary	22,000
Drawings	40,000	Interest on capital	750
Bal c/d	20,795	Profit share	40,145
	62,895		62,895
		Bal b/d	20,795

Current account: Geoff

Dr	£	Cr	£
Drawings	30,000	Bal b/d	1,800
Bal c/d	3,905	Salary	14,000
		Interest on capital	900
		Profit share	17,205
	33,905		33,905
		Bal b/d	3,905

Task 11:

Below is the statement of financial position for Joey and Tiger.

You are told that the capital balances at 31 March 2021 were:

Joey: £50,000 and Tiger £50,000

The profit for the year was £66,000 and the partners share the profits equally.

The balances on the current accounts on 1 April 2020 (start of the year) were:

Joey: £6,000 credit

Tiger: £2,000 debit

Drawings were taken during the year of:

Joey: £18,000

Tiger: £26,500

You are required to complete the "represented by" section at the bottom of the statement of financial position.

Hint:

You already have the capital account balances, but you will need to calculate the balances of the current accounts.

You might find it useful to draw the current accounts first, even though they may not be part of the question. It will help to avoid errors.

Two blank ones are here for you to use:

PARTNERSHIP APPROPRIATION STATEMENTS AND CURRENT ACCOUNTS

I have used the blank current accounts to enter the balances at the start of the year, the profit shares owed to the partners and the drawings they have already taken.

The balances from the current accounts are entered into the "represented by" section of the statement of financial position.

Current account: **Joey**

Dr	£	Cr	£
Drawings	18,000	Bal b/d	6,000
Bal c/d	21,000	Profit share	33,000
	39,000		39,000
		Bal b/d	21,000

Current account: **Tiger**

Dr	£	Cr	£
Bal b/d	2,000	Profit share	33,000
Drawings	26,500		
Bal c/d	4,500		
	33,000		33,000
		Bal b/d	4,500

Statement of Financial Position for JT Partnership at 31 March 2021

Non-current assets:	Cost	Acc. Depreciation	Carrying amount
Machinery	£80,000	£12,000	£68,000
Current assets:			
Bank	£24,000		
SLCA	£42,000		
Inventory	£15,000	£81,000	
Current liabilities:			
PLCA	£22,000		
Accruals	£ 1,500	£23,500	
Net current assets:			£57,500
Net assets:			£125,500

Represented by:

	Joey £	Tiger £	Totals £
Capital accounts	50,000	50,000	100,000
Current accounts	21,000	4,500	25,500
Totals	71,000	54,500	125,500

The capital account balances were given in the question and the current account balances were calculated from the information provided. Each are entered and totalled and the overall total will equal the net assets of the statement of financial position.

Task 12:

True or False?	True	False
Interest paid on capital balances is credited to the partners' current accounts. [true as this is owed to the partners]	√	
Profits are always shared equally between partners in the appropriation statement. [false as profits can be shared however the partners have agreed]		√
The appropriation statement follows the partnership statement of profit and loss. [true as this is drawn up below the sopl]	√	
Appropriation statements are used for sole traders and partnerships. [false as these are only used to share profits between partners]		√
Interest charged on drawings is credited to the partners' current accounts. [false as interest on drawings is charged to the partners so is debited to their current account]		√
Commission paid to partners is credited to their capital accounts. [Tricky one! False as it is credit to their current account, not capital account]		√
Current account balances appear in the 'represented by' section at the bottom of the statement of financial position. [true as this is found at the bottom of the sofp]	√	
Drawings are debited to the partners' current accounts. [true as this reduces what the partnership owes the partners]	√	
Profit shares are credited to the partners' current accounts. [true as this is money owed to the partners by the partnership]		√
A credit balance in a partner's current account represents money owed to the partner from the partnership. [true as	√	

PARTNERSHIP APPROPRIATION STATEMENTS AND CURRENT ACCOUNTS

this is a liability to the partnership]		

Task 13:

You have been provided with the following information about a partnership business.

- The partners are Ana, Will and Jordan
- The financial year end is 31 March 2021.
- The profit for the year was £78,000 before appropriations.
- The partners salaries are Ana £35,000, Will £30,000, Jordan £22,000.
- The partners interest on capital are Ana £1,000, Will £1,200, Jordan £1,500.
- The partners interest on drawings are Ana £200, Will £300, Jordan £400.
- The profit share ratio is 4:4:2.

Complete the appropriation statement below for the partnership.

Hint: If you are left with a residual loss, you need to share this in the same ratio that you would share the profit.

Note: The appropriations statements may be laid out differently, but the content is basically the same.

PARTNERSHIP APPROPRIATION STATEMENTS AND CURRENT ACCOUNTS

	Total £	Ana £	Will £	Jordan £
Profit for the year	78,000			
Salaries [deduct from the pot]	-87,000	35,000	30,000	22,000
Interest on capital [deduct from the pot]	-3,700	1,000	1,200	1,500
Interest on drawings [add back to the pot]	900	-200	-300	-400
Residual profit or loss for distribution	-11,800			
Share of residual profit or loss		-4,720	-4,720	-2,360
Total profit shared	78,000			

Check:

Totals:

Ana   £31,080

Will   £26,180

Jordan £20,740

              £78,000

Task 14:

Zoe and Ben have been in partnership for several years sharing profit equally.

The partnership agreement states that Zoe receives a salary of £20,000 and Ben receives a salary of £25,000.

Both partners receive interest on capital at 10% of their capital account balances at the year-end.

The capital balances at the year-end were: Zoe £50,000, Ben £80,000.

Zoe took out £15,000 in drawings and Ben took out £20,000 in drawings. Interest is charged on drawings at a rate of 5%.

The balances on their current accounts at the start of the year were: Zoe £3,000 credit, Ben £4,000 debit.

The profit for the year was £98,000.

a) Complete the appropriation statement below for the partnership.

Remember: The appropriation statement may be in a different format, but the content is the same.

PARTNERSHIP APPROPRIATION STATEMENTS AND CURRENT ACCOUNTS

Enter the profit for appropriation, then deduct the salaries and interest on capital from the profit.

Add back the interest on drawings.

Calculate the residual profit left for distribution and share this equally between the partners.

	Total £
Profit for the year	98,000
Interest on capital:	
Zoe	-5,000
Ben	-8,000
Salaries:	
Zoe	-20,000
Ben	-25,000
Interest on drawings:	
Zoe	750
Ben	1,000
Residual profit or loss for distribution	41,750
Profit shares:	
Zoe	20,875
Ben	20,875
Total residual profit or loss distributed	41,750

b) Complete the partners current accounts below.

Start with the opening balance of the current accounts, taking care to put them on the correct side (they could be either side).

Enter everything that the partnership owes the partners as credits.

Enter everything that the partner owes the partnership or has already taken as debits. Then balance the accounts.

Current account: Zoe

Dr	£	Cr	£
Interest on drawings	750	Bal b/d	3,000
Drawings	15,000	Salary	20,000
Bal c/d	33,125	Interest on capital	5,000
		Profit share	20,875
	48,875		48,875
		Bal b/d	33,125

Current account: Ben

Dr	£	Cr	£
Bal b/d	4,000	Salary	25,000
Interest on drawings	1,000	Interest on capital	8,000
Drawings	20,000	Profit share	20,875
Bal c/d	28,875		
	53,875		53,875
		Bal b/d	28,875

Task 15:

a) Profits of a two-person partnership are £40,000.

Total interest on capital accounts is £3,000.

Total salaries are £18,000.

If the remaining profits are shared equally, how much will each partner's share of the residual profit be?

> **Profit is £40,000.**
>
> **Deduct the interest on capital and the salaries from the profit pot.**
> £40,000 – £3,000 – £18,000 = £19,000
>
> **Profits shared equally. £19,000 / 2 = £9,500**

b) Profits of a two-person partnership are £62,000.

Total interest on capital accounts is £4,000.

Total interest on drawings is £2,500.

Total salaries are £20,000.

If the remaining profits are shared equally, how much will each partner's share of the residual profit be?

> **Profit is £62,000.**
>
> **Deduct the interest on capital and salaries from the profit pot.**
>
> **ADD back the interest on drawings.** £62,000 – £4,000 – £20,000 + £2,500 = £40,500
>
> **Profits shared equally. £40,500 / 2 = £20,250**

c) Paula and Zenildo are in partnership sharing profits and losses in the ratio of 3:2.

The opening balances in their current accounts are:

Paula: £4,000 credit

Zenildo: £1,800 debit

The profit for the year is £63,000 and there are no other appropriations.

Calculate the closing balances of the partners current accounts after the profit has been shared.

You may choose to draw up the T accounts for this one, but I have shown it in maths format. Choose what makes sense for you!

Paula
Balance £4,000 credit.
Profit share = £63,000 / 5 parts then multiplied by 3 = £37,800
£4,000 credit plus £37,800 credit = £41,800 credit

Zenildo
Balance £1,800 debit.
Profit share = £63,000 / 5 parts then multiplied by 2 = £25,200
£1,800 debit plus £25,200 credit = £23,400 credit

Task 16:

Answer the following questions in your own words.

Note:

Your answers will read differently to my answers. My answers should be used as a guide. You need to be able to write these explanations in your own words.

You will see that I start my explanations by using words from the question.

a) Explain what drawings from a partnership are.

Drawings are a record of the money or inventory that are taken out of the business by a partner.

b) Explain why interest on drawings is charged to partners.

Interest on drawings is charged to the partners to deter them from taking too much money out of the business.

c) Explain why interest on capital is paid to partners.

Interest on capital is paid to the partners to encourage them to leave their money in the business.

d) Explain why current accounts are kept for partners.

Current accounts are kept by the partnership as a record of what the partners are each owed from the business or what they owe to the business.

e) Explain what a partnership appropriation statement is for.

A partnership appropriation statement is used to distribute the profit from the business. It includes any salaries that have been agreed, any interest on capital payable to the partners, any commission owed to the partners, any interest on drawings charged to the partners. Then the balance or the residual profit is shared between the partners using the profit share ratio agreed by the partners.

f) Explain what a credit balance in a current account means for the partner.

A credit balance in a partner's current account indicates that the partner is owed money from the partnership.

g) Explain what a debit balance in a current account means for the partner.

A debit balance in a partner's current account indicates that the partner owes the partnership money.

h) Explain how a profit share ratio is decided.

The profit share ratio is decided between the partners and there is no specific way to calculate this. It is totally up to the partners and what they agree.

I hope you have found this workbook useful. If you have any comments, you can find me on my Facebook page: Teresa Clarke AAT Tutoring.

Teresa Clarke FMAAT

Printed in Great Britain
by Amazon